All About Cas

Young Learne

Keith Goodman

Published by G-L-R (Great Little Read)

Copyright: The English Reading Tree/GLR

This book is sold subject to the condition that it shall not by way of trade or otherwise be resold or hired out or otherwise circulated without the written or verbal consent of the author.

Written by Keith Goodman

Reading Age for this book: 7+

The reading age for the series starts at seven

The English Reading Tree Series has been written for children aged seven and over. It is the perfect tool for parents to get their children into the habit of reading.

This book has been created to entertain and educate young minds and is packed with information and trivia, and lots of authentic images that bring the topic alive.

TABLE OF CONTENTS

Introduction 5

Motte and Bailey 7

Why Were Castles Built? 9

The Development of the Castle 11

Life in a Medieval Castle..16

Interesting Castle Facts..21

Famous Medieval Castles 24

Castle Glossary of Terms 31

A Castle Siege 39

Thank you for Reading this Book................................45

Attributions...50

Introduction

Why were castles invented?

The golden age of castle building took place from the 11th century. Castles were a means for rulers to demonstrate their wealth and power to the local peasants.

Castles were not only built to withstand an enemy attack, but also to be the home for the local lord and his family, or the king touring his kingdom.

During the medieval period, castles were converted from wood to stone and became more advanced as defensive structures that featured round towers, barbicans and fortified gatehouses.

Let's start at the castle in its earliest form; the motte and bailey.

Motte and Bailey

The first castle design was the motte and bailey.

A motte and bailey has two main parts.

The motte is a raised piece of ground with a fortified structure on top. This structure is called a Keep.

The bailey is an enclosed courtyard that can be defended.

The motte and bailey fulfilled two prime functions. It was a home and was also a military fortress.

These motte and bailey structures were not difficult to build using the unskilled workers of the time, which were plentiful.

Even though construction was easy, they were very good at offering protection for the people inside.

Motte and bailey castles were built all over Europe from the 10th century onwards. The design was brought to England by the Normans.

A famous English motte and bailey Castle is Windsor Castle in England, although this has been added onto over the years.

By the end of the 13th century, the design was considered old-fashioned, and other types of castles were built.

Why Were Castles Built?

Castles were more than just a military base. They were centers of local government and a home for the region's leader and his family.

Castles were much smaller than military bases. Unlike the Romans, who had huge military bases and massive armies controlled by Rome, the medieval period of government was based on the feudal system.

The feudal system de-centralized power away from the king and gave it to individual lords who ruled different areas of the kingdom.

Even though the king was the figurehead of the kingdom, the real power was with the nobles, who had their own knights and soldiers.

The Lords had to provide military help to the king in times of war.

The lords built castles for their families and soldiers and ensured that the local peasants paid taxes and didn't rebel. This was the main purpose of a castle.

The Development of the Castle

Dover castle is a fine example of a stone keep castle

The construction of castles during the Middle Ages (medieval period) was fundamental to the security of kings and nobility of the time. For almost a thousand years, wood and then stone castles effectively provided protection for their inhabitants.

The Normans were prolific castle builders, and they built a massive number in England after they invaded in 1066. Even though there were already castles in England before the Norman invasion, the Normans quickly built a large number all over the country to stop the Saxons from rebelling.

The earliest type of castle that the Normans built in England was either developed inside an old Roman fort or was a motte and bailey. These were replaced by stone keep castles that, in turn, were replaced by powerful concentric castles.

Motte and Bailey

These were constructed by the Normans and had two parts. The motte and the bailey. The motte was a high hill made of compacted earth and rubble with a wooden keep (tower) on top. There was a fence around the keep.

The bailey and motte were separated by a wooden bridge that could be pulled up if the Bailey was under attack. The bailey was surrounded by a fence and a ditch filled with water. Some castles had more than one bailey. The bailey had a bridge that could be raised for added security.

The Stone Keep Castle

This type of medieval castle came after the motte and bailey and was much better equipped to fight off attackers.

The main feature of this structure was a high stone wall keep (tower) that was very thick.

There were very few windows, and entry into the keep was by stone steps.

The kitchens were on the first floor, and living spaces were on the top floor.

The first keeps were in the shape of a square, but the design was flawed because there were blind spots that attackers could use to get inside.

Designs soon changed to circular keeps.

The Bailey was outside the keep and surrounded by thick stone walls.

The castle was usually surrounded by a moat (water-filled ditch). To get into the castle, you must cross the drawbridge, which could be raised at any time.

Concentric Castles

These were built and developed in the 12th and 13th centuries and were the ultimate in castle design.

Beaumaris castle is an example of a concentric castle

The walls of the concentric castle consisted of an inner stone wall with turrets and a lower outer wall. The outer wall was built at different levels so that archers on the inner wall could fire at the enemy.

The space in the middle of the inner and outer walls was called the 'death hole' because anybody in this space faced certain death.

Like the other castles, the outer walls were enclosed within a moat, and access was across a drawbridge.

Life in a Medieval Castle

Castle Great Hall

In the Middle Ages (medieval times), castles were the homes of the rich and powerful nobles that ruled over the peasants. They were crowded, noisy places with little of the comfort we know today. There were servants, soldiers, and entertainers as well as the lord and lady with their family. Castles were homes and fortresses that kept the people inside safe from harm.

The Lord and Lady of the Castle

The owner of the castle and his family were the most important people. Sometimes these people were so powerful that they owned more than one castle. There was not much privacy within the cold walls made of stone, but at least the owners had private rooms where they could entertain visitors. All castles would also have a private chapel where the family could go to worship. The private quarters would be in the part of the castle that was the most secure.

Soldiers

Castles had soldiers. These men would patrol the walls, open and close the drawbridge and throw thieves into the dungeons. The person in charge of the soldiers was called the constable. The constable had his own room, but the soldiers slept together in a large dormitory.

More soldiers would be used from the surrounding countryside if the castle was attacked. The soldiers would be armed with swords, spears, axes, and longbows.

Even though castles were attacked, it was tough to gain entry. Normally the attackers would surround the castle and try and starve the occupants into surrendering. This could take months.

The Servants

In medieval times, the housework was done by hand, so castles were full of servants. The top servants would help the family. They helped them dress, made the fires, and served food at the table. Other servants cleaned, cooked, looked after the horses, and did the menial chores around the castle, like repairing things. For servants, the day began at sunrise and finished late in the evening. Whenever the lord entertained at a great feast, there were acrobats, jugglers, and minstrels that entertained the nobility.

Medieval castles would have been far from pleasant compared to our modern-day living standards. Not only would they have been dark and cold, but the lack of sanitation would have made them very smelly.

Life in a castle would have been focused on the Great Hall, which was a feature of every castle in England and Europe. This hall was the center for entertaining visitors and celebrations. It would have been a place to have feasts, dances, and entertainment.

The food served in a feast would have been luxurious for the time and may have included peacock, venison (deer), trout, salmon, and wild boar. The arrangement for seating in a great hall would have been according to your importance. You were considered important if you were seated close to the host family. People of less importance would have eaten at the back of the hall.

Close to the Great Hall would have been the kitchen, which would have been big and filled with cooks who prepared the food and servants that carried it to the tables.

Interesting Castle Facts

Stone fortress with bell tower

Castle comes from a Latin word that means fortress.

On average, it took about 10 years to build a castle.

The oldest European castle that is still lived in is Windsor Castle. This was built by William the Conqueror and has been used by the British Royal Family for over 900 years. The oldest standing castle is the Chateau de Doue-la-Fontaine in France. This was built in 950 A.D.

Because medieval castles were so smelly and damp, the floors were covered in straw, and sweet-smelling herbs were everywhere to mask the smells.

The spiral stairs of castles were always built clockwise. This made it very difficult for right-handed people coming up the stone stairs to swing their swords. Defenders could swing their swords with no problems.

In England alone, there are over 1,000 castles.

Dover Castle is the biggest in England, and Prague Castle is the largest in the world.

The world-famous art gallery, the Louvre, in Paris used to be a castle

Alnwick Castle in Northumberland (England) was used as Hogwarts in the Harry Potter films.

There are plenty of stories about haunted castles, and one of the most famous haunted castles is in Scotland. Edinburgh Castle has many ghosts, and one of them is a dog. The most haunted castle in the world is Leap Castle in Ireland. The locals have plenty of stories to scare the visiting tourists.

Famous Medieval Castles

There are some fantastic and stunning castles in Europe. Too many to put in one book. Here are just a few favorites. These range from Britain's medieval fortresses to some fairytale castles in Germany.

Orava Castle (Slovakia)

This castle was built on a very thin piece of rock. It was constructed to defend the area against the Mongol invasions in the 13th century. It is thought to be the most beautiful castle in Slovakia but was built when the region belonged to the Kingdom of Hungary.

Conwy Castle (Wales)

Conwy castle was built by King Edward I while he was conquering Wales between 1283 and 1287. It is thought that the castle cost around £15,000 to build, which was an extraordinary amount of money for the time. Over the next few centuries, it proved to be a very strong fortress and withstood many wars and sieges.

Conwy Castle

Edinburgh Castle (Scotland)

This castle is on a rock that is also an extinct volcano. It towers above the city of Edinburgh and has commanding views of the surrounding countryside. It is one of the oldest fortified buildings in Europe, and the rock itself was inhabited in the first century. In its 1100 years of existence, it has faced and held off many sieges. It is one of Scotland's most visited attractions.

Dunnottar Castle (Scotland)

This is a castle that was built in the medieval period. Set on top of cliffs that tower 160 feet above the sea, the castle, sadly, is now in ruins. It was once an impregnable fortress of one of Scotland's most powerful families: the Earls of Marischal. Dunnottar Castle is famous as the place where the Scottish Crown Jewels were hidden when Oliver Cromwell and his army invaded Scotland in the 17th century.

Hohenzollern Castle (Germany)

This castle sits at the top of Mount Hohenzollern and is visible from many miles away as it dominates the surrounding landscape. This is the third castle built on the site, the first being built in the 11th century. It was destroyed in 1423 after a 10-month-long siege. Since then, two other castles have been built, the last in 1846.

Hohenzollern Castle

Arundel Castle (England)

Hundreds of castles were built by the Normans after their invasion in 1066. One of the first Norman Castles in England was Arundel, which is in Norfolk and boasts a motte that is 100 feet high.

It belonged to the Dukes of Norfolk for centuries after.

The Tower of London (London)

The Tower of London (White Tower) was built by William the Conqueror in 1078 and is famous all over the planet. It controlled

London and served as a palace, but over the years has been used as a prison and the home of the crown jewels.

These days it is one of the biggest tourist attractions in London.

Bodiam Castle (England)

The castle was constructed in 1385 in the county of East Sussex.

It was a moated castle, but even though it looks impressive was not ideally situated or built to withstand an attack. The walls were too thin, and it was too small to house a significant number of defenders.

Windsor Castle (England)

Windsor is one of the oldest and biggest castles in England. It was built by that prolific castle builder, William the Conqueror.

The castle is still used as one of the residences of the Royal Family.

Warwick Castle (England)

Another castle was built by William the Conqueror.

This one was constructed in 1068 and was used by the Normans to keep the Anglo-Saxons from revolting.

It was built near the River Avon and was the residence of the Earl of Warwick until King Henry II took it in the 12th century. King Edward IV was imprisoned here in 1469 during the Wars of the Roses.

The castle was one of the most secure fortifications in medieval times.

Alhambra Palace of Granada (Spain)

In Spain, one of the features of the castles is that Muslim invaders built many, so the architecture is magnificently different.

When the threat from Muslim invaders was no longer relevant, the castles were taken over by Spanish nobility and did not serve a military purpose.

Alhambra (Grenada)

However, examples like the Alhambra Palace are breathtakingly beautiful.

Castle Glossary of Terms

Battlements on a tower with Arrowslits in the walls

Arrowslits

Castle Arrowslits were narrow holes in the wall that allowed bowmen to fire arrows at attackers. They were angled for better vision and could also be used for a bolt from a crossbow.

The Castle Barbican

A barbican is a fortified structure that protects the gatehouse against attack. This was the castle's first line of defense and could be used in several ways. One such way would be to close a gate behind the enemy soldiers and trap them in the enclosed space. The defending archers could then rain down arrows on them. Small castles would have two towers in the barbican, while large castles could have four.

Battlements

This is a walking space at the top of a castle wall that has openings for firing arrows or pouring hot oil over an attacking enemy. The function of a battlement is to give the defenders of a castle or city something to hide behind and space to return fire.

The Drawbridge

One way of defending a castle was to have a water-filled moat (ditch) all around the building. A drawbridge went over the water to allow people to come in or out. The drawbridge could be pulled up if the castle was attacked. Drawbridges were made of wood and were attached to pulleys and winches that enabled them to be lowered or raised very quickly.

The Dungeon

A stairway or a secret passage led underground to the castle dungeon. This was where political or religious prisoners were kept captive. Dungeons were miserable, extremely damp, and cold, with hardly any light. They were designed to drive a prisoner mad.

The Gatehouse

The entrance into a castle was the most vulnerable part, but medieval castle builders used barbicans and other devices to make the gatehouse (entrance) very strong. The space to enter a castle through the gatehouse was always narrow so it could be defended more efficiently. The portcullis was a heavy grilled gate made of metal or heavy oak. It was suspended by ropes above the entrance and could quickly be lowered.

The gatehouse would have a portcullis at both ends of the passage, and the attackers would be trapped inside by dropping both. The defenders were then free to pour boiling oil on them or fire arrows.

The Castle Keep

In the early stages of castle development, castle keeps were built in wood. Later, stone was used.

The keep was the most important place in the castle. Castle keeps could be placed on higher ground than other parts of the castle.

This was the case with the Motte and Bailey design. In the early medieval period, the lord and his family would live in the keep.

As castles became grander, the family lived in more comfortable places, and the keep became just a fortified defensive tower.

Castle Machicolations

The word is French and means 'to crush.' They jutted out from the castle wall and were used to drop rocks and boiling oil on attackers.

The Castle Moat

A moat is a ditch that is filled with water. A drawbridge going across could be raised in case of danger.

Portcullis

The portcullis is a heavy wooden or metal grill suspended above the castle entrance. It could be dropped very quickly if the castle was attacked.

Ramparts

The rampart was the defensive boundary of a castle. A bank made from earth and stone protected the early medieval castle. Ramparts could be manmade, natural, or a bit of both. Thick stone walls were built on top of the ramparts to make them more difficult to attack.

Castle Towers

One of the main areas for the defense of a castle was the tower. They were built in various shapes, although the most popular were either circular or square.

The tower was used to fire arrows at attackers, and it could also be used to store things and put prisoners.

Circular towers were more practical as they gave better vision to the defenders, and there were no blind spots that attackers could use.

Castle Turrets

A turret is not the same as a tower as it is not free-standing. A turret is attached to a tower or a wall. A tower is built from the ground up, but a turret comes out from another structure. Turrets are smaller than towers.

Castle Walls

The walls of a medieval castle changed drastically over the years and became much stronger.

In the early medieval period, they were simple mud and stone structures.

As the medieval period progressed, they were constructed of thick stones connected with towers.

The walls were wide enough for soldiers to get quickly to parts of the castle that were under attack.

Castle Watchtowers

Medieval watchtowers were built very high to help people in the castle to have a good view of the surrounding land.

A Castle Siege

Catapult

If an invading army wanted to take over an area protected by a castle, the castle would have to be overcome. This gave the leader of the army a huge problem. Trying to attack the wall would mean that many soldiers would be killed without any guarantee of success.

The aim of a siege was to starve the defenders by stopping the supply of food and water. It was hoped that the people inside would eventually surrender. A siege could last days, weeks, months, or even years, depending on how well supplied the defenders were with food, water and weapons. Access to water was vital.

Most castle sieges ended with victory for the attackers.

As well as the lack of food and drink, illness and disease could play a massive part in the outcome of a siege. Remember, in those days, sanitation was primitive and medical knowledge practically nonexistent.

The attackers used trebuchets (form of catapult), which hurled large rocks at the castle's walls. Flaming pieces of wood could also be thrown to make fires inside the walls. As well as the trebuchets, there were smaller, more maneuverable catapults that could throw small rocks at the defenders on the battlements.

The weakest part of a castle was the main gate and drawbridge. Attackers would use hooks to try and pull the drawbridge down.

As well as throwing large rocks at the castle walls, an attacking army could try to dig underneath them or light fires underneath to make the walls collapse. This would not be possible if the castle had a moat.

Battering rams were used to make holes in the walls or the main gate. These battering rams were large and had covers to give the soldiers some protection, though not that much. The battering ram was usually a big tree trunk with a pointed metal end. It would be rammed repeatedly against the gate or wall.

Battering Ram

Attacking troops would use ladders to get over the walls, but a more sophisticated way was to use a siege tower. The siege tower would be pushed against the castle wall and held in place with grappling hooks.

When faced with a castle that had a moat, the siege became more difficult though not impossible.

The attackers could take time and build a bridge or get across on barges.

For an attacking army, archers were crucial, and they would fire thousands of arrows into the air onto the defenders.

Crossbowmen were also used like modern-day snipers.

During the medieval period, a good archer could fire 12 arrows a minute.

These arrows could be set on fire to create havoc inside the castle.

Defending a castle

If the right decisions had been made when the castle was built, it would be in the ideal location to withstand an attack.

It would generally be on a hill or mountain and have a moat. If it were built on rock, it would be impossible for anyone to dig under the walls.

With the development of the canon the walls castles were easy to destroy

High, thick castle walls made of stone would make it difficult for attacking soldiers to get in, and having a barbican to protect the gatehouse would be extra security.

A castle needed good supplies of food, water, and weapons to fight off a long siege.

The drawbridge would be raised at the first sign of an attack and the portcullis lowered.

Soldiers defending the castle would be on the battlements. They would fire arrows, drop rocks, and pour boiling oil on attackers.

It would have been difficult for an attacking army to get over the walls of a castle, and many soldiers would have died in the attempt. It was far better to surround the castle and wait for the defenders to surrender.

With improvements in weapons and the use of canons, castles became less effective in stopping an attacking army, and they stopped being safe places to run to.

Thank you for Reading this Book

You can visit the English Reading Tree Page by clicking:

Visit Amazon's Keith Goodman Page (Mailing List)

Books in the Young Learner series

All About the Anglo Saxons

All About the Titanic

All About the Battle of the Little Bighorn

All About the Second World War

All About the American Revolutionary War

All About American History

All About George Washington

All About the Normans

All About Japan

All About Stonehenge

All About Castles

All About the Hundred Years' War

Some of the Books in the English Reading Tree Series by Keith Goodman include:

The Titanic for Kids

Shark Facts for Kids

Solar System Facts for Kids

Dinosaur Facts for Kids

American Facts and Trivia for Kids

My Titanic Adventure for Kids

Discovering Ancient Egypt for Kids

Native American Culture for Kids

Meet the Presidents for Kids

The American Civil War Explained for Kids

The American Revolution Explained for Kids

World War One in Brief for Kids

World War Two Explained for Kids

Colonial America for Kids

Middle Ages Facts and Trivia for kids

The Cold War Explained for Kids

The Wild West and Stuff for Kids

The Great Depression and Stuff for Kids

Early American History for Kids

Awesome Alabama for Kids

Twentieth-Century America for Kids

American Democracy Explained for Kids

Amazing Alaska for Kids

America at War for Kids

Titanic Conspiracy Theories for Kids

Famous Americans for Kids

Twentieth Century Heroes and Villains for Kids

Wild West History for Kids

The French Revolution Explained for Kids

Key events that created America

The Bermuda Triangle Mystery for Kids

The Russian Revolution Explained for Kids

UFO Mysteries for Kids

America in the 1970s for Kids

America in the 1980s for Kids

America in the 1940s for Kids

America in the 1990s for Kids

America in the 1930s for Kids

America in the 1920s for Kids

Chinese Dynasties for Kids for Kids

America from 1910 to 1919 for Kids

1917 for Kids

The Titanic Diary for Kids

Myths and Legends for Kids

The Loch Ness Monster for Kids

The Vietnam War for Kids

Attributions

Xastle Author ccaetano Standard licence
https://depositphotos.com/ID 5874784

Motte and bailey Author Fotografiche Standard licence
https://depositphotos.com/ID 193870182

Medieval castle Author mproduction Standard licence
https://depositphotos.com/ID 12176817

Dover castle Author RPBMedia Standard licence
https://depositphotos.com/ID 622537184

Beaumaris castle Author suzbah Standard licence
https://depositphotos.com/ID 41557831

Banquet hall Author Ravven Standard licence
https://depositphotos.com/ID 222590220

Stone fortress Author Nikol85 Standard licence
https://depositphotos.com/ID 292095426

Orava castle Author nahlik Standard licence
https://depositphotos.com/ID 295206088

Conway castle Author samot Standard licence
https://depositphotos.com/ID 56988273

Hohenzollern Castle Author Maugli Standard licence
https://depositphotos.com/ID 177330506

Alhambra Palace Author vidarnm Standard licence
https://depositphotos.com/ID 319132814

Battlements Author ValeriHadeev Standard licence
https://depositphotos.com/ID 230738668

Castle Author ValeriHadeev Standard licence
https://depositphotos.com/ID 230738668

Castle towers Author ValeriHadeev Standard licence
https://depositphotos.com/ID 230738668

Watchtower Author ValeriHadeev Standard licence
https://depositphotos.com/ID 230738668

Catapult Author jamesgroup Standard licence
https://depositphotos.com/ ID 19082745

Battering Ram Author 3drenderings Standard licence
https://depositphotos.com/ ID 25672569

Canon Author Sonulkaster Standard licence
https://depositphotos.com/ ID 511564740

Printed in Great Britain
by Amazon